Walking
in WESSEX

Twenty seasonal walks
in Wiltshire

Nick Channer

WESSEX BOOKS
SALISBURY . WILTSHIRE

Ashton Keynes has many delightful stone buildings (Walk 5)

Published in the United Kingdom in 2016 by Wessex Books

Text © Nick Channer 2016

Design and layout © Wessex Books 2016

Cover artwork by KFD Ltd

Edited by Jane Drake
Wessex Books, 10 Thistlebarrow Road, Salisbury Wilts SP1 3RU
Tel: 01722 349695
Email: info@wessexbooks.co.uk
www.wessexbooks.co.uk

Printed in India

ISBN 978-1-903035-47-4

The publishers cannot accept responsibility for errors or omissions,
or for changes to details included in the text. All the walks described in
this book were field-checked prior to publication.

On the route south of Chitterne. (Walk 2)

Contents

Preamble

When Britain's walking guide industry was an entirely new concept, most books concentrated on walks that were best suited to the months covering the period from late spring to early autumn. True, this is when the weather is likely to be at its best, the temperatures are generally more agreeable and the daylight hours are longer. But to preclude the depths of winter is to deny readers ideas and suggestions for walking in what can be one of the loveliest and most atmospheric of the English seasons.

This walking guide to Wiltshire redresses the balance by offering twenty circuits in the county that reflect the best of spring, summer, autumn and winter. They are walks that can be completed at any time of the year though some are better suited to a particular season. This is emphasized in the chapter introduction.

At the heart of Thomas Hardy's Wessex, Wiltshire is one of the south of England's's loveliest counties, incorporating many familiar aspects of our unique countryside. The region's history is long and eventful and its many archaeological sites are a fascinating legacy of ancient times. There are extensive areas of forest and woodland, picturesque river valleys, pretty villages, grand country houses and idyllic water meadows - a rich and diverse landscape waiting to be explored on foot.

Walking through the seasons in Wiltshire offers the chance to search for bluebell woods and daffodils in spring; to enjoy the natural beauty and breathless hush of the countryside on a perfect summer's day, marvel at the glorious spectacle of autumn colours in the leafier parts of the county; and savour the thrill of a frosty morning on the downs in winter.

In the main, you don't have to be a serious rambler to tackle the walks in this guide. However, there are sometimes patches of wet ground to be found – even on a short walk – and some of the routes cross low-lying ground and lush water meadows, which are prone to flooding. Therefore, appropriate footwear is always an important consideration when out walking. A camera and a small rucksack to carry rainwear are also recommended and a copy of the relevant OS map is essential, especially if you want to extend the walk. Details are provided in each chapter. Several of the walks start at or near railway stations so you might want to consider the train as an alternative means of getting to the start of the circuit.

Several routes pass through land managed by the Forestry Commission and therefore in some cases the walk is over permitted paths, rather than statutory rights of way. Please remember that these are working forests and tree felling and other work may necessitate the route of the walk being diverted in places. Clear signs indicate where operations are taking place. Two walks, at Stourhead and Stonehenge, are over land managed by the National Trust and English Heritage. Bear in mind that in some instances the route is over permitted paths and may be subject to diversions or closures.

Finally, I hope you enjoy walking through the seasons in this grand county, which always looks as if it evolved with the walker in mind.

Nick Channer

Heading towards
The Cursus (Walk 17)

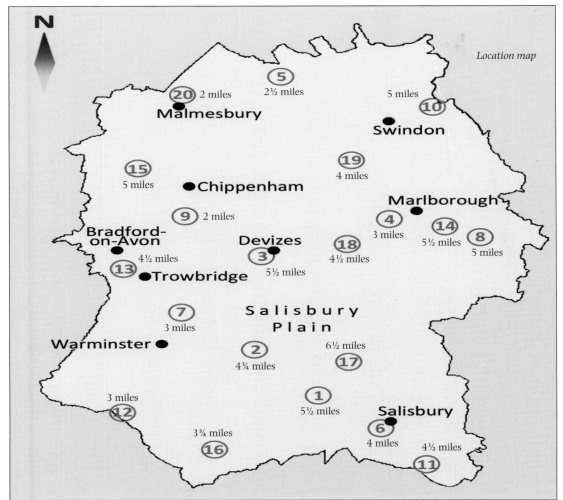

Location map

N

(5) 2½ miles

(20) 2 miles

Malmesbury

5 miles

(10)

Swindon

(15)

5 miles

●Chippenham

(19)
4 miles

Marlborough ●

(9) 2 miles

Bradford-
on-Avon ●
4½ miles

(13)

Devizes
(3) ●

(4)
3 miles

(14)
5½ miles

(8)
5 miles

(18)
4½ miles

Trowbridge

5½ miles

Salisbury
Plain

(7)
3 miles

Warminster ●

(2)
4¾ miles

6½ miles

(17)

(1)
5½ miles

Salisbury

(6)

3 miles

(12)

3¾ miles

(16)

4 miles

4½ miles

(11)

1. Great Wishford

...os and Parking

...ys and byways in the
...steady climbing on the
...ard leg with several quite
...ep ascents.

The Royal Oak at Great
Wishford is a delightful old pub,
ideally located just before the
finish of the walk.

The walk starts in Great
Wishford, just off the A36
between Salisbury and
Warminster. Parking is usually
available in South Street, in the
centre of the village
(GR SU081353).

Following a Royal Escape Route

In addition to striking, far-reaching views there is plenty of flora and fauna on this very attractive walk. Spring is a good time to complete it, as everything is bursting into life and glorious hazy carpets of bluebells can be seen through the trees. It's also a good walk in autumn when the beeches are at their best, dazzling the eye as far as you can see. At the heart of the route is Grovely Wood, which is managed for forestry and wildlife and perfect for exploring on foot. The walk's return leg follows a stretch of the Monarch's Way, a long-distance trail tracing Charles II's escape route after the Battle of Worcester in 1651.

The Walk

1 With your back to the church, walk down **South Street**, passing the **Old Post House** on the right. Until recent times this was the site of the village stores and post office. Keep left at the next main junction, just past **Grovely Cottages** and Oak View. Turn right after a few paces onto a bridleway and immediately you pass under the Salisbury to Warminster railway line.

2 Follow the track between fields, climbing steadily towards **Grovely Wood**. Avoid a track on the right and keep ahead on the restricted byway. Continue the steady climb between fences and the going becomes harder as the track runs between trees and bushes. It's worth pausing for a short break when you reach a seat on the left. From this vantage point there are impressive views over woodland and chalk downland, and glancing back down the track towards **Great Wishford**, you should be able to glimpse the tower of the village church framed by trees and protected by a very English landscape of fields and woodland rising around it. Keep climbing and then on the level ground the track passes through woodland. Soon the walk encounters another steepish climb before levelling out to reach a major junction with a broad avenue of beech trees.

3 In front of you is a bridleway running south. Avoid this and turn right along the avenue. There are glimpses of fields and open downland over to the left. Eventually, just beyond a barrier, the avenue swings right. Leave it at this point and walk straight ahead, following a clear woodland path. On reaching a lane turn right, following the long-distance **Monarch's Way** now. Extensive carpets of bluebells can be seen beside the route, usually around early May. Pass a triangular junction and continue on the long-distance trail. Don't take the permissive bridleway further on; instead, keep to the Monarch's Way.

Bluebells dazzle the eye in Grovely Wood

4 Pass a small parking area on the right and, beyond the woodland, follow the lane through a long, dry valley, heading towards **Great Wishford**. Pass a barn on the left and some distance further on, the walk once more passes beneath the railway. Just beyond it is the **Royal Oak** on the outskirts of the village. Keep ahead to within sight of the church and turn right immediately before it to return to **South Street** where the walk began.

Th...
Child...
Socie...

What to look out for

In the wall outside Great Wishford church are what are known as the **bread stones.** These tablets indicate the price of a gallon of bread from the Napoleonic Wars onwards. At the start of the 19th century, England and France were at loggerheads; the French blockaded this country and as a result prices soared. The parish was badly affected, with villagers forced to pay 8d more for bread than other communities. In an effort to reassure other residents that the asking price was genuine, the local baker recorded his price in stone in the churchyard wall and the tradition has been maintained ever since.

Looking back to Great Wishford

In the unlikely event that you are in Great Wishford at dawn on 29th May – **Oak Apple Day** – don't be surprised to find the villagers dressed in period costume, banging tin pans and accompanied by traditional musicians. Armed with billhooks, they set off on foot for Grovely Wood where they gather fallen and dead wood and cut an oak bough, which is then decorated with ribbons and hung from the church tower in the village. This ancient custom has its origins in pre-Christian tree worship and also involves residents processing to Salisbury Cathedral, where at the steps of the high altar, they proclaim their rights, chanting: 'Grovely, Grovely and all Grovely! Unity is strength.'

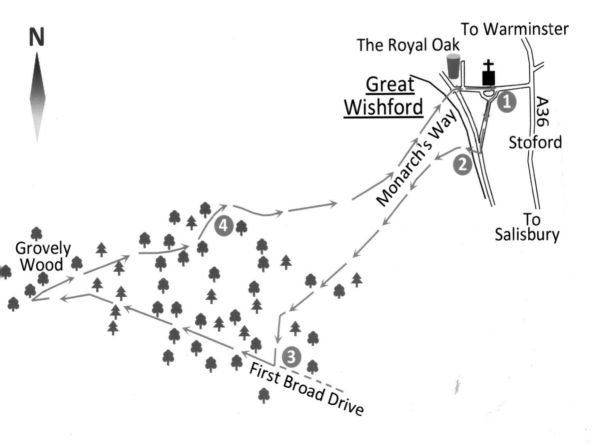

2. Chitterne

Paths, Pubs and Parking

Initially on roadside and pavement, then tracks and paths. There is no pavement after Chitterne on the first stretch along the B390 and although there are sometimes long gaps when there is no traffic, it can also get relatively busy; take extra care, keeping to the right-hand edge of the road and walk in single file. The final stage of the walk is along a quiet country road. Some gentle ascents and descents but no steep climbs.

The King's Head at Chitterne is a rambling stone building ideally placed almost at the end of the walk.

The walk starts at Chitterne on the southern edge of Salisbury Plain, on the B390 Heytesbury to Shrewton road. Park in the vicinity of the church, just off the main road in the village centre (GR ST993441).

The Silent World of Salisbury Plain

This is a walk with a tangible sense of drama and adventure. The route, which should only be attempted by more experienced walkers, begins by exploring the village of Chitterne and then leaves the B390 to cross open country; the sound of traffic quickly recedes as you enter a world of stillness and solitude. Heading west across the southern edge of Salisbury Plain, the views from the walk are consistently magnificent and are without doubt some of the most memorable in Wiltshire.

The Walk

1 With your back to the church, turn left and walk along to the T-junction. Turn left towards **Amesbury** and follow the B390 uphill through **Chitterne**. There are sections of pavement either side of the road. At the top of the village, pass a turning on the right for **Chitterne Dairy** and keep ahead. Beyond it, where the pavement ends, proceed with caution along the right-hand side of the road, passing the Chitterne village sign.

2 Look for a bridleway and gate on the right and head up the field towards trees. To the right here is a glorious view of Salisbury Plain stretching to the horizon and nestling in the dip is **Chitterne church**, surrounded by trees and rooftops, creating a delightful picture that is typical of this wonderful county. As you approach trees on the far side of the field, bear left and join a perimeter track, following it as it curves right. More grand views open up to your left, this time over towards Stonehenge and neighbouring Hampshire.

3 On reaching a major intersection of tracks and a bridleway post, turn right and follow the track beside an old triangulation pillar on the right. These were originally placed in the landscape to define high ground but have now been superseded by more advanced satellite technology. Ahead are glorious westerly views – rolling downland in the vicinity of the Wylye valley and the county's boundary with Dorset. Make for woodland, where there is another waymark, cross a track and continue heading west. Keep the trees on your immediate right and beyond them walk ahead down the gentle slope, the scene dominated by a stunning landscape in front of you.

On the route south of Chitterne

Everywhere you look, there are vast swathes of downland peppered with belts of woodland. Continue down the track; when trees block your route, go a few paces to the left of them and cross a primitive stile. Keep ahead with trees on the right. At the corner of the fence, continue down the field slope, making for a gate by a junction.

4 Join the road by a sign for **Codford Dairy**, turn left and walk the short distance to a gate and waymark on the right. Go diagonally down the field, following an obvious route through crops to the next gate and continue across a meadow to a footbridge and a gate beyond it. Pass through it and up the field slope towards trees and a gate

in the boundary. Once through the gate, turn right along a metalled farm lane and make for the next gate. Just beyond it the lane sweeps left. As it does so, keep right along the field edge, initially with hedgerow hard by you on the right. Leave the hedge and stride out across the middle of the field, maintaining the same direction, towards a gate in the distance. Go through the gate and continue ahead on the path, following it along the field edge. There are trees on the right. Keep going, making for a stile on the right at the end of the trees. Cross over and bear right to a footbridge. Continue ahead for a short distance to a stile and join the road.

5 Turn left and follow the public highway, essentially quiet along this stretch. The buildings of **Chitterne** can be seen in the distance. At the T-junction, near the **King's Head**, turn right and walk along to where the road bends right. Turn left here and return to the church where the walk started.

What to look out for

When you think of **Salisbury Plain** the image that comes to mind is usually that of an undulating chalk plateau, a hostile, desolate place with much evidence of military activity and more than a hint of ancient mystery. The depths of winter can be a good time to explore the public rights of way here if you like your walking to be dramatic, demanding and unpredictable, but a walk in this region on a sunny spring day is an altogether different experience – and usually a very rewarding one. Salisbury Plain and the whole of North Wessex were once the most heavily populated areas in the country, inhabited by the people of the late Stone Age and Bronze Age. Ironically, today, in this small, overcrowded island of ours, the 300-square-mile Plain is one of the loneliest and least populated tracts of land in the south of England – if not all of Britain.

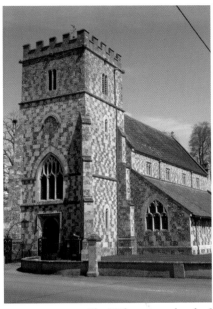

The 19th-century church of All Saints with St Mary, Chitterne

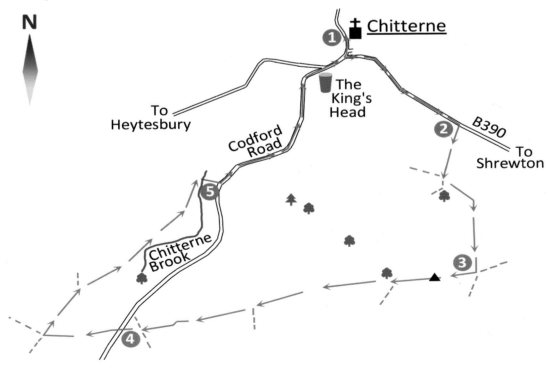

3. Devizes

Paths, Pubs and Parking

Towpath, pavement and byways.

There is plenty of choice for food and drink in Devizes. In the vicinity of the Market Place are various cafes and watering holes, including the Black Swan, and nearby are the Crown and the Castle Hotel in New Park Street.

Devizes lies to the north of Salisbury Plain. The walk begins in the fee-paying car park at Devizes Wharf Centre by the Kennet & Avon Canal (GR SU005617).

On a Town and Country Trail

This is a walk packed with surprises and perfect for any season, though spring is certainly one of the best times when many of the fields outside Devizes are bright yellow with oil seed rape and the trees lining Quakers' Walk are bursting into leaf. There is a real sense of renewed vigour and hopefully a hint of summer on the way as you explore this fine mix of town and country. Beginning by the **Kennet & Avon Canal**, the route heads for the edge of town and then into open country before changing course and returning to Devizes, this time to the heart of the town for a heritage trail that includes some of its numerous listed buildings.

The Walk

1 From the car park by the **Kennet & Avon Canal** make for the towpath and turn right, passing beneath the bridge **(number 140)**. Follow the towpath briefly and at the next bridge, leave the canalside and cross over to join **Quakers' Walk**, passing a cottage with the remains of a well in the garden. Continue along the tree-lined path, all the way to the next road. Ahead is the outline of **Roundway Hill**, a local landmark popular with walkers. One of Wiltshire's famous chalk horses can also be seen, carved into the hillside.

2 Turn right and follow **Roundway Park** to the A361. Turn right to the crossing, go over the road and after a few paces take the turning for the **Kennet & Avon Canal**. On the left is the entrance to **Brickham House**. Cross the canal and turn left down to the towpath. Follow it ahead to **Coate Bridge**, completed in 1990. At this point leave the towpath, cross **Windsor Drive** and take the lane opposite, signposted **Coate**. Along here are very pleasant stretches of Wiltshire downland in the distance.

3 Turn right after about 100 yards to follow a byway, part of the **Wessex Ridgeway**, cutting between trees, hedgerows and banks of vegetation. Begin climbing and after a few paces take an obvious path on the left. Keep on the path and in late spring bluebells are seen here among the trees – but only briefly. At length you reach a junction with another byway. Turn right by a corrugated barn and head up the slope. On this stretch the **Vale of Pewsey** and the **White Horse at Alton Barnes** are visible. There are also good downland views to the south. Continue over a footpath crossing and on reaching the next track intersection, turn right. Follow the track and now the rooftops of Devizes peep into view. Approaching the outskirts of the town, pass **Nursteed Community Primary School** on the left. At the roundabout go straight over into Brickley Lane and follow the road to the next main junction (mini roundabout).

4 Turn right along **Brickley Lane** and at the next island, keep left to follow **Jump Farm Road**. Along here is an interesting blend of architectural styles – from striking brick villas to Edwardian terraces. As you approach **St James's church** and the junction with **London Road**, turn left into **Church Walk**. Pass a pond, known as the **Crammer**, and make for the pedestrian crossing at the next road. Continue across **The Green**, a delightful unspoiled corner of Devizes. Merge with the road by some picturesque cottages and keep ahead at the mini roundabout by **Pans Lane**.

The view from the churchyard of St John the Baptist

5 At the next junction turn right into **Long Street**. Head back towards the town centre, passing lines of handsome houses and quaint cottages. On the left is the **Wiltshire Heritage Museum**. Turn left at the footpath sign by the entrance to the churchyard of **St John the Baptist**. Follow the path as it bends right after a few paces, along the churchyard boundary. From here there is a striking glimpse of **Devizes Castle** among the trees. On reaching some wrought iron gates turn right into **St John's Court**. Look out for **Number 4** on the left, a medieval hall. **Devizes Town Hall** is ahead of you by the junction and on the right is the Lamb, one of the town's older pubs and totally unspoiled. Keep ahead, with the Town Hall on your right and the **Silk Mercer pub** on the left.

Oil seed rape adds a touch of brightness near Devizes

6 Proceed into the **Market Place** and on the left is the historic 16th-century **Bear Hotel**. Keep ahead into **Northgate Street** and at the next junction, turn right by the **Wadworth Brewery** into **New Park Street**. Pass the Crown and then turn left at the sign for **Devizes Wharf Centre**. Return to the car park at the start of the walk.

What to look out for

Devizes Wharf has been much improved in recent years. Signs of industry have gone and today the Kennet & Avon towpath is part of an attractive scene enhanced by a former granary, which now houses a canal museum. **Devizes is one of Wiltshire's prettiest towns**. Round every corner and in virtually every street there is something of note to catch the eye. Many of the town's famous listed buildings are to be found in and around the spacious Market Place. In the late 1960s this corner of Devizes was used in the filming of the Thomas Hardy classic *Far from the Madding Crowd*, starring Peter Finch and Julie Christie and directed by John Schlesinger.

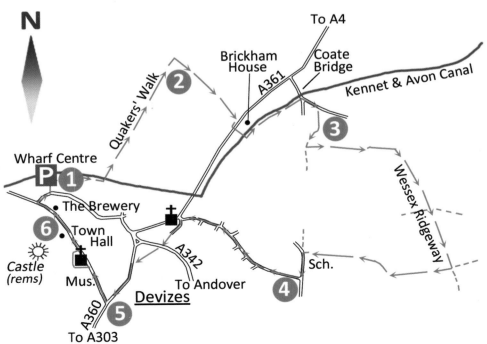

4. West Woods and Lockeridge

Paths, Pubs and Parking

Moderate climbs, obvious tracks and meandering paths within West Woods (be prepared for very muddy sections after prolonged rain).

The Who'd a Thought It pub at Lockeridge lies about half a mile from the route of the walk (see point 2). There is also a picnic area at the walk's starting point.

The walk begins at Clatford Bottom, part of West Woods, south of the A4 to the west of Marlborough. There is a Forestry Commission car park at the start of the walk (GR SU163667).

Signs of Spring in West Woods

Apart from an optional spur to the village of Lockeridge, where there is a welcome pub, almost all this pretty walk is under cover of trees. The focus of the route is West Woods, comprising about 600 acres of mainly beech woodland and renowned throughout the area for their wild daffodils and hazy carpets of bluebells in spring. Beginning at Clatford Bottom, the walk explores the eastern half of West Woods, following the popular Wansdyke Path for the last leg.

The Walk

1 From the car park turn left and walk along the track towards the road for about 120 yards to a barrier on the right and a bridleway on the left. Take the latter route through the vegetation to a gate and go slightly left in the field, up the grassy slope towards trees. Make for a gate and bear right in the woodland. Keep to the obvious tracks and paths, following the waymarks. Head down steeply to a junction and go straight over to a path, descending quite steeply. Cross over a wide path and at the next junction keep left for a few paces to a waymarked T-junction. Turn right for about 50 yards to a major intersection with a field and fence in front of you.

2 Bear left, initially following the footpath along the edge of the woods, with the pasture on your right. Continue deeper into the woodland, heading diagonally up through the trees to a track. To visit the **Who'd a Thought It pub**, turn right, make for a gate and barrier and at the road go straight on, down to a junction. Cross over, follow the lane down into the centre of **Lockeridge** and at the next junction turn right for the pub. To continue the main walk, turn left and proceed down the track, following it as it sweeps right. Avoid a path running off sharp left here and continue through **West Woods**. Glancing to your right along this stretch reveals brief glimpses of **Forest Lodge** beyond the trees. Draw level with the building and then reach a waymarked intersection in the heart of the woods. Continue ahead for about 75 yards to the next junction and keep left here, still following a track.

Springtime at Lockeridge

3 Head uphill and when the main route sweeps left at a hairpin bend, go straight on, following a rough track. Continue heading up the slope towards the edge of the woods and when you reach a junction, avoid a path running along the woodland edge and keep left along a waymarked bridleway (**Wansdyke Path**), heading deep into West Woods again.

4 On reaching a junction with a track, keep left for about 50 yards, then bear right, still following a waymarked bridleway. Pass over a path intersection and continue on the bridleway. Keep ahead at the next signposted junction and descend to meet a track. Turn left and down below among the trees you can spot the car park where the walk began. Several paths thread through the trees to reach it.

What to look out for

The **Wansdyke Path** is 14 miles long and runs from Marlborough to Morgans Hill near Calne. The Wansdyke itself consists of a single bank and ditch and was probably constructed by the Britons as a line of defence against the Saxons.

The Who'd a Thought It pub

The Britons lived south of the line, the Saxons to the north of it. Other sections of the defence can still be traced between Marlborough and Bristol. Looking at what remains of the Wansdyke today – a low, crumbling, grassy bank in the shade of the trees – it is hard to believe that it could ever have served a useful purpose. The density of the surrounding woodland and the close proximity of the trees belie the strategic importance of its former role as a vital frontier.

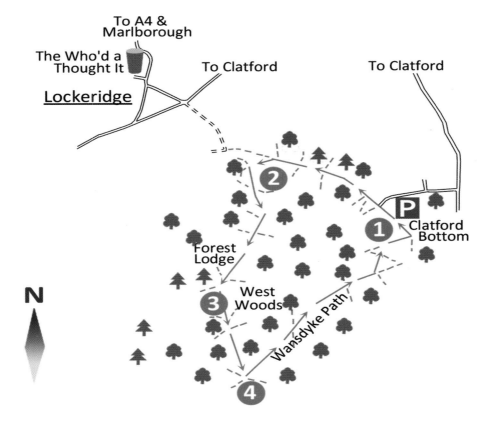

5. Ashton Keynes

Paths, Pubs and Parking

Village streets, well-surfaced paths and several fields and meadows. The going is flat and easy from start to finish.

The White Hart in Ashton Keynes is a short distance from the start of the walk.

The village lies between the A429 and the A419, in the north of Wiltshire, close to the border with Gloucestershire. The car park, where the walk begins, is by the recreation ground in Ashton Keynes (GR SU047937).

A Village Tour by the Trickling Thames

The name Ashton Keynes means 'the farm where the ash tree grows' and the village is one of the prettiest in this delightful northerly corner of Wiltshire. With its charming stone houses and intricate maze of streets, there is a definite hint of the Cotswolds about it. Wherever you stroll within the village, water is never very far away and just outside Ashton Keynes, frequent winner of the Best Kept Village Award, lie the extensive lakes of the Cotswold Water Park. From the recreation ground car park, this undemanding walk – very much a village tour – makes for the parish church of Holy Cross, its churchyard festooned with daffodils and blossom during the weeks of spring. It is here that the route appears to be playing tricks on the walker. Just when you think you are turning your back on picturesque Ashton Keynes and making for open country, another hidden corner of the village reveals itself. Eventually, you head away from lines of quaint cottages and handsome houses towards fields and lakes, but only briefly before returning to the start.

The Walk

1 From the car park turn right and walk beside the road and the **infant Thames** towards the **White Hart**. Turn left into **Gosditch** and walk between houses and cottages, passing the village primary school on the right. At the next junction turn right and follow the pavement to a stile. Here you have a choice. Either continue on the road, the next stage of which doesn't have a pavement, or cross the stile and follow the footpath, which runs roughly parallel. Cross two further stiles to a drive, turn left and follow the path beside perimeter fencing, rejoining the road at **Sheepwash Bridge**. Continue to **Holy Cross church**.

2 Go through the churchyard to a gate and follow a path beside several seats and a line of trees. Pass through the next gate and join the riverbank at a pretty spot on the walk. Several stone houses overlook the water here and the scene is delightfully calm and tranquil. Pass **Glebe House** on the left before reaching the next junction. Swing left and then right into **Back Street**, pass **Richmond Court** on the right and on the left now is striking **Plough House**, originally a pub. On the right is **The Leaze**, a residential development. Continue between period houses and modern infilling and follow the road as it bends right beyond **Pilgrim Cottage**. Just after the bend look for a **Thames Path** waymark and turn left.

The churchyard of Holy Cross church is full of colour in springtime

3 Follow the track for about 70 yards and then veer right to a kissing gate. Go through it and head along an enclosed path skirting a meadow. Make for the next kissing gate in the corner, turn left and follow the **Thames Path** between houses to the road. Cross over and follow the national trail across a drive and then across the village playing field. Pass the pavilion on the right and go through a gate by a sign for **Ashton Keynes Millennium Green**. Keep to the right edge of the next field, pass through trees and make for another gate and a second Millennium Green sign. Continue for about 40 yards towards lakes, then turn right and follow the path as it sweeps right to a stile.

4 Go diagonally across two fields to reach the road on a junction. Turn left, avoid the road on your immediate left and walk ahead into **Ashton Keynes**, passing **Honeysuckle Cottage** on the left just before the next junction. On the right is the village recreation ground with the car park beyond it.

What to look out for

The stone-edged **Thames**, Britain's most celebrated river, divides into

Ashton Keynes has many delightful stone buildings

several channels at **Ashton Keynes**, navigating its way through the village en route to London. Here the Thames is only 7 miles from its source and little more than a swirling stream. Glancing down at the water as you make your way through Ashton Keynes, it is hard to believe this is the same river that flows so majestically through the capital on its way to meet the sea. If you're looking to attempt something a bit more ambitious than a short village walk, you could try the **Thames Path**, a 180-mile long-distance trail following the course of the river from its source to the **Thames Barrier**. The route never strays far from the riverbank and the scenery is a wonderful mix of superb architecture, varied wildlife and colourful boating activity - England at its best.

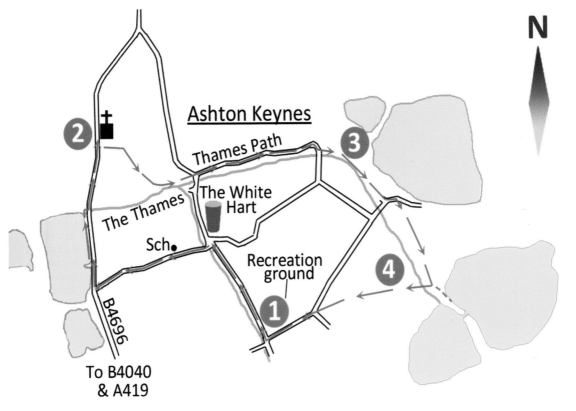

6. Salisbury

Paths, Pubs and Parking

Easy, level walking with a mixture of urban pavements and rural paths.

There are numerous pubs, restaurants and coffee shops in Salisbury. The Old Mill Hotel and Inn at Harnham, directly on the route of the walk near where it finishes, dates back to 1135 and was converted in 1550 to provide Wiltshire's first paper mill.

The walk starts at Harnham, just to the south of Salisbury, on the A3094. There is a small car park in the village (GR SU136291). An alternative option would be to travel to Salisbury by train and join the walk between points 3 and 4.

Magical Meadows and a Soaring Spire

This gentle and undemanding walk along the River Nadder to the city's cathedral offers plenty to catch the eye and capture the imagination. By starting outside Salisbury, it avoids the thorny problem of parking and yet takes you to the very heart of this ancient and beautiful city. Stroll by the Avon and visit the magnificent Close before beginning the return leg across the famous water meadows. The stunning view from here of the cathedral's graceful spire was immortalized by Constable in his classic painting.

The Walk

1 From the car park turn right and briefly follow **Harnham Road**. Veer right into **Lower Street**, passing the car park of **St George's church** on the left, and continue along the road. Avoid **Town Path** on the right and walk ahead along **Middle Street**. Pass the aptly named **Constable Way** and make for Middle Street Meadow on the right. This native wildflower meadow lies between the houses of **Harnham** and the banks of the **Nadder**.

2 Leave the road at the meadow entrance, by a bungalow (number 34), bear left and follow its boundary hedge with a football pitch over to the right. Look for a gap in the hedge as you reach the end of the pitch and rejoin the road. Turn right and walk along to **Upper Street**. As it swings left, join a clear and obvious path (signposted **Bemerton**). The path soon divides; take either route and follow it through woodland to a wooden footbridge.

3 Keep right here, cross the **Nadder** and follow the enclosed path between fields, meadows and trees, heading towards Salisbury. Cross a wooden footbridge by a house with solar panels and head for several more bridges beneath trees. On reaching the entrances to **Fitzgerald Farm** and **Bridge House**, turn right and follow the road towards the city centre. There are some striking gabled villas and terrace houses on the left. Cross **Cherry Orchard Lane** and follow **Churchfields Road**. On the right are garages, car showrooms and industrial units. Pass more houses before reaching a roundabout. Salisbury railway station is to the left.

The Avon flowing through Salisbury

4 Turn right here and pass the entrance to **Fisherton Island**. The road soon reaches a row of detached villas on the left. Keep right at this point and follow the path, avoiding the footbridge over the Nadder on the right. With the river on your right, make for a footbridge ahead. The bridge crosses a feeder stream. Once across it turn right and take the riverside path along to the confluence of the **Nadder** and the **Avon**. Keep left and follow the waterside path along to the next road bridge.

5 Turn right here, following **Crane Street** to the junction with **High**

Street. Turn right here and walk along to **Salisbury Cathedral** and the **Close**. Retrace your steps along **Crane Street** to the bridge and follow the picturesque riverside path by the Avon and Nadder to the second footbridge. Cross it and follow **Town Path** across the meadows towards **Harnham**. Watch out for cyclists approaching from behind, often unseen and unheard. Cross a bridge by **Rose Cottage** and pass the **Old Mill Hotel and Inn**. Continue ahead along the road, turn left at **Lower Street** and return to the car park.

The Old Mill at Harnham

What to look out for

Salisbury Cathedral was begun in 1220 and completed around 1280, although the 404-ft spire wasn't added until 1334. The Cloister and Chapter House, which contains a medieval frieze and an original copy of the 1215 Magna Carta, date back to 1280. Among many fascinating features worthy of closer inspection in and around the Close is Malmesbury House, which Handel used for his recitals and where Charles II stayed at the time of the Great Plague.

Thomas Hardy loved Salisbury. 'The Close of Salisbury under the full summer moon on a windless night is as beautiful a scene as any I know in England or, for the matter of that, elsewhere,' he wrote. The city became the inspiration for Melchester, which appears in some of Hardy's novels, including *Jude the Obscure*. In the book, Jude works as a stonemason on the cathedral.

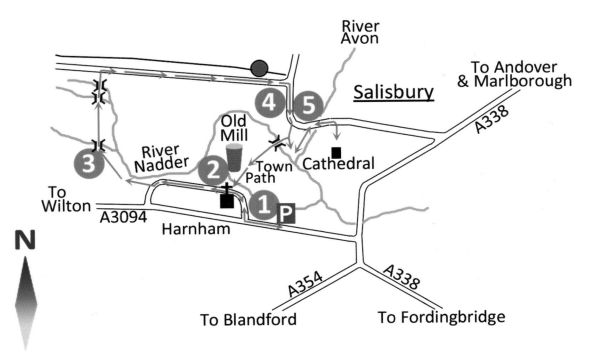

7. Bratton

Paths, Pubs and Parking

From the road at Bratton, an initial and lengthy climb to Bratton Camp, followed by high-level tracks and paths descending gradually to Bratton church and the village.

The Duke at Bratton, only a few yards from the car park where the walk starts, is a traditional 18th-century pub that was once three cottages.

The village of Bratton is on the B3098 on the northern edge of Salisbury Plain. The walk begins in the car park in Tynings Lane (GR ST914523).

Breezy Walking and Beautiful Views

The contrast on this excellent walk is stunning. At the start you are exploring Bratton, a typical Wiltshire village; before long you are climbing steeply to Bratton Camp, one of the county's ancient hill forts. The route's next objective is another of Wiltshire's magnificent carved white horses. This one, the Westbury White Horse, lies just yards away as you battle your way along a downland path above the figure on what has to be one of the county's highest and breeziest walks. The return leg offers tantalizing glimpses of Salisbury Plain, a sinister and mysterious landscape, and the distinctive tower of Bratton's 13th-century church in the distance.

The Walk

1 From the car park, walk along **Tynings Lane** to the junction with the B3098. Nearby is the **Duke pub**. Keep left and walk through **Bratton**, passing several turnings. On reaching the edge of the village, bear left onto **Castle Road**. Begin a moderate climb; over to the right is a good view of the chimney at Westbury's locally famous cement works, a striking and very useful navigational landmark. Further up you pass over a bridleway crossing the road. Continue ascending, the climb becoming steeper.

2 When the road curves left, veer half right over a stile and round to the right. Keep to the right-hand edge of **Bratton Camp**. The 25-acre site includes a long barrow burial mound probably constructed before 3,000 BC. Follow the grassy perimeter to the point where a flight of steps becomes visible. Follow them down to a lower path, which is immediately above the figure of the **Westbury White Horse**. Turn left and the scene here is dominated by dramatic views towards **Westbury Hill**. Walk along to a gate and ahead is a car park. Turn left and follow the access road, which is also a byway, to a T-junction. Turn right and head south on the byway to a junction by the buildings of **White Horse Farm**. Ahead lies the vast expanse of Salisbury Plain.

3 Turn left at the junction and follow the **Wessex Ridgeway**. Pass a track with a 'Keep Out' sign on the right and walk along to a bridleway on the left. Take the turning and immediately after the third gate swing right to a fourth gate and follow the path between fencing. Go through a fifth gate and follow the fencing. The tower of Bratton's **St James the Great church** can be seen in the distance.

4 On reaching an arrow on a fence post, head diagonally down the escarpment towards the church. At the bottom pass through some trees and drop down to a kissing gate. Follow a woodland path to the next junction and keep left, heading down beside the churchyard.

Heading towards Bratton church

Pass the entrance, go down and then up a flight of steps, cross a lane and continue on the path to the next road. Turn right and return to the centre of **Bratton** where the walk began.

What to look out for

The **Westbury White Horse** is Wiltshire's oldest chalk figure. 180-ft long, 108-ft high and dating back to 1778, this white horse is believed to have replaced a much earlier figure cut in celebration of King Alfred's victory over the Danes in AD 878. The Westbury White Horse is best appreciated from a distance, as are all the county's chalk figures.

On the downland above Bratton

Bratton church is one of Wiltshire's finest buildings. Its setting is also highly impressive, standing amid trees and set against a striking downland backdrop. The architecture is well worth a closer look too. The 15th-century tower has grinning gargoyles and a stair turret, the arcades rest on clustered columns and the north transept has angels playing musical instruments or carrying shields.

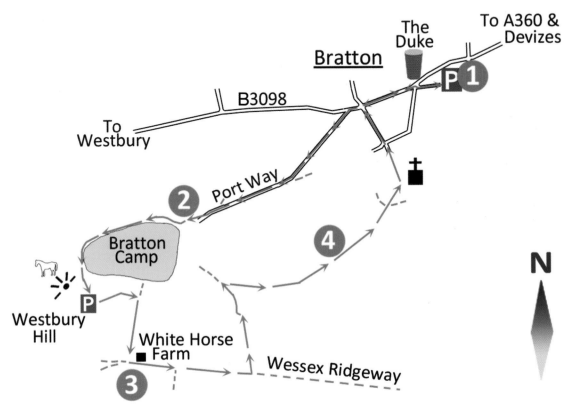

8. Great Bedwyn

Paths, Pubs and Parking

Towpath, field and woodland paths with several stretches of quiet road.

There are two pubs on this walk, the Cross Keys and the Three Tuns, and both of them are near the start and finish point in Great Bedwyn. There is also a café at Crofton Pumping Station, midway round the circuit.

The village lies between the A338 and the A346, south of the A4, not far from Marlborough and Hungerford. The car park by the Kennet & Avon Canal, on the edge of Great Bedwyn. represents the walk's starting point (GR SU281644).

Steam Ahead at Crofton

One of the pleasures of the great outdoors in high summer is a walk along one of Britain's historic inland waterways – perhaps early in the evening, when there is still warmth in the air after the day's long hours of sunshine. A visit to a nearby pub for a rewarding drink is also a strong incentive. In Wiltshire it is the Kennet & Avon Canal to which walkers flock for such an experience and the stretch between Great Bedwyn and Crofton, the outward leg of this walk, is hard to beat for tranquility and attractive scenery. At Crofton, the route leaves the towpath and meanders across country via farmland and woodland, back to the start at Great Bedwyn.

The Walk

1 The starting point for the walk is the site of the old **Great Bedwyn wharf**. Coal would have been transported here from the Somerset Coal Canal. From the car park, head west, keeping the waterway on your right. Follow the towpath and the church of **St Mary the Virgin** can be seen on the opposite bank. Continue on the towpath, following it all the way to **Crofton**. Cross over at the lock near the pumping station. Pass beneath the railway and through Crofton's grounds to the main gate. Turn right. *When the pumping station at Crofton is closed, continue west on the canal towpath to the next road bridge, cross it, keep right and follow the lane beside the waterway. Resume the main walk when you reach the entrance to the pumping station.*

2 From the pumping station, follow the lane between trees, fields and hedgerows. When it bends right, turn left at the sign for **Crofton Farm** and follow the course of a Roman road north between farm outbuildings. Continue between fields with views of woodland, pass a corrugated barn on the left and soon afterwards turn right to follow a byway. Keep to the field edge, heading towards trees. Over to the right you can see the Kennet valley.

3 Enter woodland via a gate in the corner and follow the track ahead, keeping right at several intersections. Eventually you come to a T-junction with a cottage visible ahead. Turn right here and follow the path through the trees. The woodland narrows to a strip; continue to a footpath sign on the left. Take the path, crossing the field towards the right-hand edge of a curtain of trees.

A rural scene outside Great Bedwyn

4 Make for the right-hand corner and look for a junction with a grassy path. Keep right and follow it east between fields into the valley, heading towards **Great Bedwyn**. There is fencing on the left. Keep ahead when the path becomes enclosed and at the road turn left and then left again at the next junction. Walk through the village, passing the historic 11th-century church, and at the junction in the centre of **Great Bedwyn**, turn right and return to the canalside car park where the walk started.

What to look out for

Completed in 1810, the 87-mile **Kennet & Avon Canal** took sixteen years to construct. The final bill was in the region of £1 million. With 104 locks and numerous other awesome features, the canal is regarded as a jewel of 18th-and 19th-century engineering. It was built to provide a direct trade link between London and Bristol, thus avoiding the treacherous south coast route. The Kennet & Avon eventually became redundant, thanks to the nationalization of Britain's railway network in the late 1940s. However, the canal's dedicated supporters were determined to ensure it wouldn't die. Restored over many years, the waterway was eventually re-opened by Her Majesty the Queen at Devizes in the summer of 1990.

The historic Kennet & Avon Canal in high summer

Designed by Boulton and Watt and re-opened by John Betjeman in 1970, following major restoration work, **Crofton Pumping Station** pumps water from nearby Wilton Water, a reservoir covering 8 acres and rising from natural springs, to the summit level of the canal. Superseded by electricity in 1958, the 19th-century beam engines are well worth a visit. Crofton Pumping Station is open from 10.30am until 5pm between Easter and around the end of September.

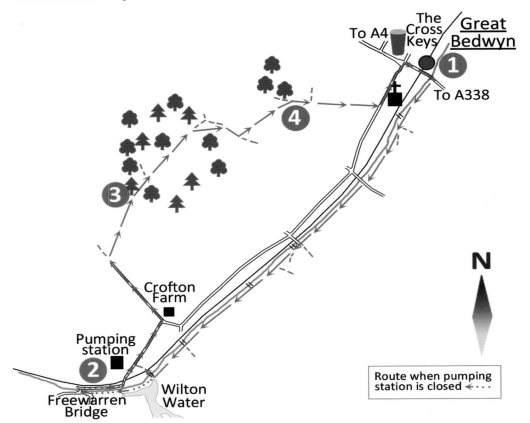

9. Lacock

Pavements, field paths and brief stretches of road. Be prepared for wet patches in the meadows by the River Avon after heavy rain.

There are several tearooms and pubs in Lacock, including the Red Lion in the High Street.

Lacock is just off the A350 Melksham to Chippenham road. The walk starts in the village's main National Trust car park (GR ST916684). There is a fee for non-NT members.

A Luscious English Landscape

Lacock is one of Wiltshire's loveliest villages, a perfect example of medieval England. With its timber buildings, jumble of gabled roofs and maze of quaint streets, there is much to catch the eye. But Lacock is not just another picture postcard village. This one is owned by the National Trust and famous for its historic abbey, founded in 1232 for Augustinian nuns. In summer Lacock's streets throng with tourists but follow this short walk out of the village and along the banks of the River Avon and you soon witness the English countryside at its glorious best – especially on a warm sunny day when the landscape shimmers in the heat, the river sparkles and the water meadows dazzle the eye.

The Walk

1 From the car park, make for the main exit, cross the road and follow the woodland path through to **Lacock**. At the road turn left and walk into the village, passing the entrance to **Lacock Abbey** and the **Fox Talbot Museum**. On reaching the Red Lion, turn right and follow **East Street** to the **Lacock Bakery**. Turn right at the junction, keeping the **Carpenters Arms** on the right. Head towards the church and turn left in front of the main gate by a house called **Nethercote**. Walk down to a packhorse bridge and a ford, avoiding a left-hand path. Continue up the lane by some cottages and when you reach a sign 'Turning point only – no parking' turn right through a kissing gate and follow the obvious path across pastures towards several cottages at **Reybridge**. Follow the path between them to the road and head straight on for a few paces.

2 Take the next right-hand turning and follow the road across the Avon. Once clear of it, cross the stile on the right and head diagonally across the meadows, with an extensively wooded hillside rising to meet the skyline over to the left. When the path meets the riverbank follow it beside the Avon to a kissing gate by some trees and continue ahead. Further on the river bends right; at this point go straight on, up to a stile. Follow the grassy path between fields, pass through a gap in the trees and hedgerow and proceed ahead in the next pasture, keeping to the right-hand boundary. Make for a stile, cross over and in front of you now is a vast meadow with **Lacock Abbey** seen over to the right. Immediately, the path divides. Keep right and head for a stone bridge on the far side of the meadow. Make for the waymark just to the left of the bridge and turn right at the road.

3 Cross the bridge; there is no pavement but room to walk along the verge. After a few paces follow an enclosed causeway with impressive views across a pastoral, typically English landscape bisected by one of the county's best-loved rivers – the Avon. At the end of the causeway,

Historic Lacock

turn left across the road to a stile and follow a grassy path diagonally across the field towards a line of trees. On reaching a stile and gate, cross into the National Trust car park where the walk finishes.

What to look out for

Lacock Abbey, which lies directly on the route of the walk, was converted to a house in the 16th century. Later it passed by marriage to the Talbot family. William Henry Fox Talbot, one of the early pioneers of photography, is buried in the cemetery in West Street. The National Trust owns both the Abbey and the Fox Talbot Museum of Photography.

The meandering Avon

If you've never been to Lacock before, you might recognize it as the **backdrop to several big-screen films and television dramas**. The village featured in the BBC adaptation of Jane Austen's *Pride and Prejudice* in 1996 when it became the fictional home of Elizabeth Bennet and her family. Very few changes were required for the filming, though the main street was covered with turf and gravel for a week and the postbox was disguised as the village pump. In more recent years Lacock was used in the making of the internationally renowned Harry Potter film series and the popular BBC costume drama *Cranford*.

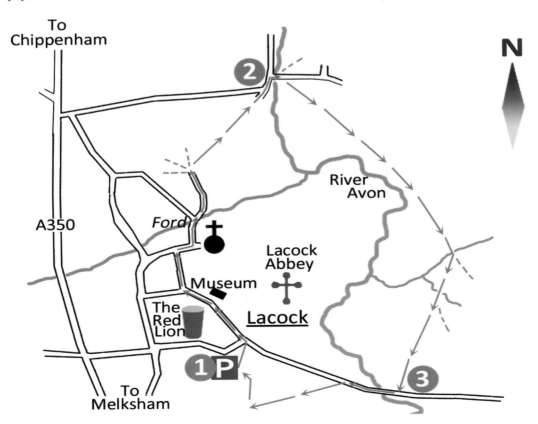

10. South Marston

Paths, Pubs and Parking

Level tracks and paths, field boundaries and village outskirts.

The Carriers Arms in South Marston lies close to the start of the circuit. There is a picnic area at Nightingale Wood early on in the walk and light refreshments are available at Roves Farm, also on the outward leg.

South Marston is off the A420, between Swindon and Faringdon. There is a car park in the village centre, adjacent to the playing field (GR SU194878).

A Literary Landscape

From the centre of South Marston, this enjoyable and very varied walk heads across country and through sprawling woodland to Roves Farm, a popular visitor attraction. From there the route follows a lengthy stretch of farm track to the village of Sevenhampton before returning to the start across a pastoral landscape of fields, trees and hedgerows. The bustling, ever-expanding town of Swindon is only a stone's throw away but the walk's surroundings are so tranquil and undisturbed, you feel you are at the heart of rural Wiltshire.

The Walk

1 From the car park turn right and follow the road to **Nightingale Lane**. Turn left and walk along to **Sevor Farm**. Swing right at the signs for **Nightingale Wood** and follow a broad track to a parking area. Walk through to the far end by some tables and benches and then head straight on, following the waymarked **Nightingale Walk**. Make for a junction by a sign for **River Cole** and **Roves Farm Walk** and turn left. Turn right after about 75 yards (The Nightingale Cycle Ride) and after several paces turn left to join a bridleway. When the track sweeps left to buildings, continue ahead, cross a path and head for the next T-junction.

2 Turn left here, heading for the outbuildings of **Roves Farm**, a popular visitor attraction. Expect to see children enjoying tractor rides in the vicinity of the farm complex. Pass the buildings and continue on the track, with the parkland of **Sevenhampton Place** seen over to the right. Walk as far as the road at **Sevenhampton**, keep right and turn right after a few paces to visit the churchyard. Ian Fleming's grave is on the left as you enter. Return to the access road for Roves Farm and beyond the houses of Sevenhampton take the path on the right for **South Marston**.

3 Go through three kissing gates and then slightly left in the third field. Make for a kissing gate in the top boundary and follow the left edge of the pasture. Pass through another kissing gate in the corner. Cross a footbridge and walk ahead on a permissive path around the edge of the field. On reaching a gap in the hedge in the far corner, turn left and immediately cross a ditch. Just beyond it turn right along a grassy track. When the trees on the left thin, look for a waymark pointing ahead. A few paces beyond it, at a wire fence corner on the left of the track, cross over and go diagonally across the field.

The view from Sevenhampton church

4 Look for a gate in the hedge to the left of trees and follow the path in a southerly direction, keeping to the right edge of farmland. Over halfway along the boundary turn right over a stile, walk ahead to a hedge and keep it on your left. Follow the path to a stile near the field corner, just beyond a pond. Cross over and, avoiding the field corner and a wide gateway over to your left, follow a straight line across the bottom of the pasture to the next corner where you reach a footbridge and kissing gate. Go through the gate and keep right, round the field perimeter, passing rows of solar panels on the left beyond wire fencing. Further down the field, look for a gate in the right-hand boundary. Go through it and turn immediately left. Head down the field and in the bottom corner, keep right for several steps, then turn left. Pass through a gate, turn left and skirt the paddock. Pass behind some outbuildings, then through a gate and turn left to cross a footbridge. Follow the path to within sight of the church at **South Marston** and the car park where the walk began is just across the road.

Four-legged residents of South Marston

What to look out for

Two very different writers crop up on this delightful walk. One is the little-known poet **Alfred Williams** who was born at Cambria Cottage near the Carriers Arms in South Marston in 1877. He worked at the Great Western Railway Works in Swindon and became known as the Hammerman Poet. Williams died in poverty in 1930. The other is **Ian Fleming** (1908-64), creator of James Bond, the world's best-known secret agent. Fleming, whose own life reads like something from the pages of a 007 novel, lived at Sevenhampton Place, near the route of the walk, and is buried in the local churchyard.

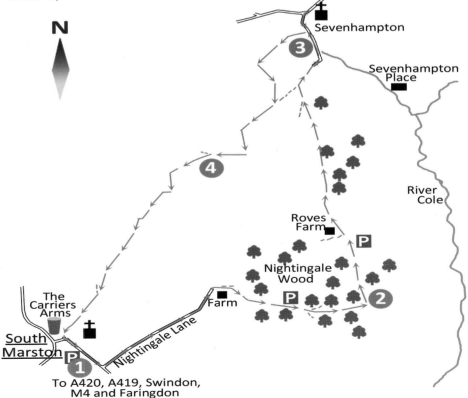

11. Downton

Paths, Pubs and Parking

Flat, level paths and tracks. Can be wet and muddy in places where you cross the Avon.

The White Horse in Downton is ideally placed at the walk's start and finish point.

The village is on the B3080, off the A338 to the south of Salisbury. The general area at the front of the White Horse, at the western end of Downton, is ideal for parking (GR SU174214).

Ambling by the Avon

From the centre of Downton, a large village which could almost pass for a small town such is the size of this sprawling community, this very enjoyable riverside walk makes for a private estate with a fascinating history. Beyond it the route takes on a delightful, water-based theme with a foaming weir and sluice and streams and meandering channels threading their way through a marshy landscape clogged with reed beds. The Avon – one of Wiltshire's prettiest rivers – is never far away as you return to Downton and the trees lining it conspire to create a glorious richly-coloured mosaic in autumn.

The Walk

1 With your back to the **White Horse pub**, turn right and walk through the village of **Downton**. Cross the **River Avon** and continue to the turning for the **church of St Laurence**. Approach the lychgate and keep right, following the path beside the church hall car park to **Barford Lane**.

2 Turn left and head north out of **Downton**, passing the cemetery and the **Catholic church of the Good Shepherd and Our Blessed Lady Queen of Angels**. Cut between pastures and hedgerows and just before the road bends sharp right, veer off to the left to follow a track across the fields. Pass over an intersection, with **Trafalgar Fisheries** on the left, go through a gate and continue ahead. Eventually you approach a lodge set against some trees. Make for a gate and stile and turn left to pass beside the lodge. Pass the Nelson chapel on the right and follow the concrete track as it bends left down to the Avon. Swing right here, by a mill cottage, and take the riverside path across a sluice and weir. Follow the obvious path across the marshes and between reed beds. Cross two more footbridges and keep ahead over the water meadows.

3 Approaching a clump of trees, veer left at a fork towards a galvanized gate by some semi-detached houses on the left side of the field. Cross a track and follow the path ahead across the pasture. Go through several galvanized gates; at the third join a concrete track and continue ahead. Keep to the track and when it swings round towards a large house and outbuildings, turn left over a footbridge and veer right. Now follow the track (**Avon Valley Path**) south towards **Downton**. The Avon lies over to the left. As you approach the village, the path makes for the riverbank, passing through a kissing gate. On reaching the road bridge, turn right and return to the parking area near the White Horse where the walk began.

The Avon – one of Wiltshire's prettiest rivers

What to look out for

For many years **Downton** was an important centre of industry and commerce. Lace became a cottage industry here and the village has long been associated with flour-milling and paper-making. Handmade paper was produced at **Downton** until the end of the First World War. Along the street, to the east of the Avon, lies the impressive former tannery building, built by the Southern Trading Company in 1919. At the rear of it was a waterwheel, ten feet in diameter.

North of Downton, and directly on the route of the walk, lies a **redundant chapel**, which is closely associated with Britain's greatest seafaring hero, Admiral Viscount Nelson. Near to the

Heading back to Downton

chapel is 18th century Trafalgar House, originally known as Standlynch House, which was acquired by the Treasury and given to Nelson's heirs in gratitude for his services. The house was later occupied by his brother, the 1st Earl Nelson, when the name changed from Standlynch to Trafalgar. The Nelson family sold the estate to the Duke of Leeds in 1948 when the annuity paid to the Nelson family by the government was terminated. The now-abandoned building, rebuilt in 1677 and dedicated for use by the Roman Catholic faith in 1914, became the Nelson family's private chapel.

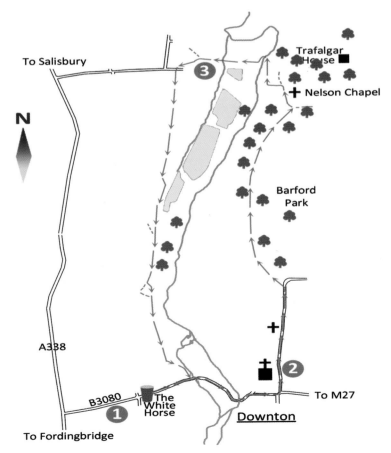

12. Stourton

Paths, Pubs and Parking

Undulating parkland; one steep climb.

The Spread Eagle at Stourton, which was given to the National Trust in 1947, lies close to the start of the walk. There is also a restaurant by the National Trust visitor entrance to Stourhead.

Stourton is on the Wiltshire/Somerset border, to the north of the A303, just off the B3092 Frome road. The walk begins at the National Trust car park in the village (GR ST779340). There is a fee payable for non-NT members.

One of the Wonders of Wiltshire

The landscape gardens at Stourhead, where this superb walk begins, are regarded as among the finest in the country – and rightly so. The gardens were designed and laid out by Henry Hoare in the 18th century. Among the buildings are the Pantheon and the Temple of Flora, two examples of architecture at its most graceful. The lakes – which date from 1448 – the mystical grottoes, the temples and the various shrubs and rare trees feature in countless guidebooks, calendars and postcards. From the National Trust car park at Stourton, the route crosses the Stourhead estate, which extends to 2,650 acres. During the walk, which explores a fine mix of woodland and parkland, there are constant views of the sprawling estate, as well as glimpses of the magnificent gardens, described by an early magazine as a 'living work of art' when the site first opened in the 1740s.

The Walk

1 From the car park make for the visitor entrance to **Stourhead**, keep left and follow the path down to the **Spread Eagle Inn** in **Stourton**. This avoids walking from the car park into the village on the road. From the **Spread Eagle** follow the road. On the right is the entrance to **Stourhead Gardens**. The **River Stour** rises here and just beside the road is the medieval **Bristol High Cross**. Originally, it stood in the centre of Bristol before being moved to Stourhead in 1765. The upper and lower niches contain statues of King John, Henry III, Edward III and Henry VI, among others. Follow the road and on the right are teasing glimpses of the famous tree-fringed lake. Pass through the **Rock Arch** and turn immediately right at the footpath to 'Alfred's Tower – 2 miles.'

2 On the left now is **Turner's Paddock and Waterwheel**. This is the site of a water pumping station built in the late-19th and early 20th century and which played a key role in supplying water to the Stourhead estate. Keep left when you eventually reach the entrance to **Beech Cottage** and follow the track to a gate and stile. Avoid the **Stour Valley Way** signposted to the right and keep right at the next fork (signposted '**Alfred's Tower**').

Stourhead's renowned landscaped gardens

Continue along the trail until you reach a junction with a red arrow (denoting a walk around the estate) and a horse trail sign.

3 Take the path and climb steeply. On the higher ground a forest track looms into view. Turn left here to a gate and the Iron Age hill fort at **Park Hill**. Avoid the stile and keep right along the path to a track. Turn right and look for a path running sharp left down through the trees. Cross a stile, where you can see **St Peter's Well** up to your left. Turn right and keep the lake on your right as you walk diagonally across the valley floor, heading uphill to a gate on the edge of woodland. Continue

ahead to a gate and turn immediately left up the bank. At this stage of the walk an obelisk, dating back to 1839, edges into view.

4 Some 150 yards beyond the obelisk, turn right onto a track and walk along to a cattle-grid and kissing gate. At the next junction of tracks just beyond them, turn right and pass in front of **Stourhead House**. Follow the drive to the road and take the path opposite, back to the car park where the walk started.

What to look out for

Autumn is without doubt the best time to visit Stourhead. Every year reveals countless colour combinations, though the russet and golden hues are inherent and remain all year round. The silver maples are almost always the first of the trees to change when autumn comes. Then it is the turn of the native beech and oaks.

The Bristol High Cross on the Stourhead estate

Alfred's Tower is a redbrick structure rising to 160 ft and considered one of the finest in the country. The windowless tower was built for the impressive view from the top, and to mark the spot where Alfred the Great erected his standard against Danish invaders in AD 879. The spire, hit by an aircraft in the Second World War, was eventually replaced in 1985. To extend the walk and visit Alfred's Tower, use the OS Explorer map and follow the waymarks.

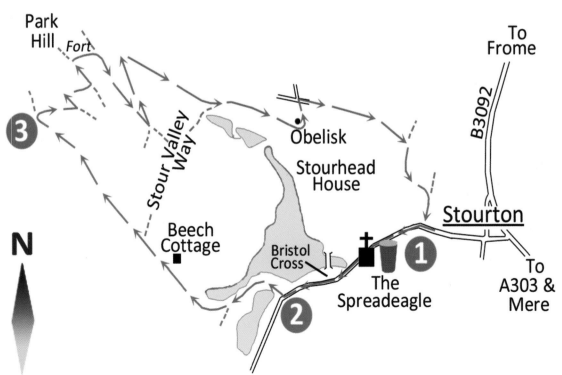

13. Limpley Stoke

Grand Views and a Classic Canal

The wooded Avon valley in all its splendour is the thread running through this delightfully scenic walk. From Limpley Stoke village the route follows the towpath of the Kennet & Avon Canal, with the River Avon parallel across the fields, as far as John Rennie's classic 19th century masterpiece, the Dundas Aqueduct, which, with its Bath stone façade and fine Doric columns, blends perfectly into this spectacular landscape. From the waterway the walk climbs steeply through woods to reach the road where there are impressive views. Eventually, you reach the picturesque village of Winsley before descending into the valley once more. The return leg to Limpley Stoke is along a further stretch of canal towpath. Here and in the initial stages by the waterway the trees look stunning in the autumn sunshine.

The Walk

1 From the front of the **Hop Pole** turn left and walk down the lane, keeping the railway on the right. Turn right at the main road and pass beneath the railway bridge. Follow the B3108, crossing the Avon at **Stokeford Bridge**, and go on uphill as far as the bridge over the **Kennet & Avon Canal**. Turn left here, joining the towpath, and follow the waterway in a northerly direction. As you progress along the towpath, note that the opposite bank of the canal is well wooded, while to the left there are excellent views across the valley towards Limpley Stoke and the Avon. Pass some timber sheds as the canal bears left and almost at once the splendid **Dundas Aqueduct** edges into view, its graceful classical design adding a touch of elegance to the restored waterway.

2 Further along the towpath is a lift bridge at the junction with the delightfully named **Somerset Coal Canal**. Bear right in line with the Kennet & Avon and pass the remains of **Dundas Wharf**. Continue along the towpath as far as the footbridge, cross the canal at this point and turn right, ignoring the route to **Claverton**. The arches of the Dundas Aqueduct can be seen through the trees. Follow the towpath high above the Avon and the railway. Looking north at this stage reveals a splendid vista along the valley floor towards wooded hills rising up in the distance. A left hand path, descending the bank via a flight of wooden steps, provides the opportunity to gaze up at the aqueduct. You need to walk a few yards over the water meadows in order to appreciate the full splendour of the mighty structure. Return to the top path and when the canal swings right, go straight on to join a path running up into **Conkwell Wood**. Climb a stile at the start and proceed up the steep hillside to a second stile and junction. Turn right by a wire fence and follow the path to the road.

3 Continue ahead, following it round a left bend and past **Copt Oak** and **Little Park**. From the gateway beyond the latter there are splendid rural views. Make for a bend by **Conkwell Grange**, go through a gap in the wall on the left and cross the field to the next boundary. Pass into the next field and keep ahead to the exit in the far right corner. Go out to a lane and turn right. At the junction, on the outskirts of **Winsley**, turn right and pass a left turning (**Late Broads**). At the next junction turn left into **Limpley Stoke Road**. Pass the Methodist church and when the road bends left towards the **Seven Stars pub**, take the right turning (signposted **Village Hall**).

The Kennet & Avon canal at Winsley

4 At a junction in front of some gates turn right and after a few paces turn right to join a path running between stone walls. Descend some steps, keeping left at the fork just beyond them. The path plunges into the valley by a series of more steps and either side of you are houses and gardens. Cross a track and continue down to a kissing gate. Go through it into a field and make for the next boundary. On reaching it, join a track and turn right, crossing a bridge to the far bank of the canal. Turn right to join the towpath.

The Dundas Aqueduct

5 This stretch of the waterway is particularly attractive, as it meanders beside wooded banks. Pass several houses and cottages, some with gardens running down to the water's edge. Later on, the houses of **Limpley Stoke** loom through the trees. Pass under the road bridge, leave the towpath and rejoin the B3108. Walk down towards the railway bridge and look out for the remains of **Limpley Stoke railway station** and sign across the valley. Pass under the bridge again and turn left to return to the start of the walk.

What to look out for

The Somerset Coal Canal opened in 1881. Part of it was restored in 1986-88 for moorings and boat base. Look for a quote from **Admiral Dundas**, Chairman of the Kennet & Avon Canal Company, dated 1845: 'We are on the most friendly terms with the Somerset Coal Canal...I trust we shall go hand in hand with them...'

Much of the area where the walk is located was used in the filming of the classic Ealing comedy *The Titfield Thunderbolt* (1952) in which the scheming owner of a coach company plots to bring down a local steam train service. A seven-mile stretch of the former Limpley Stoke and Camerton line is the setting for the Titfield-Mallingford branch line in the story.

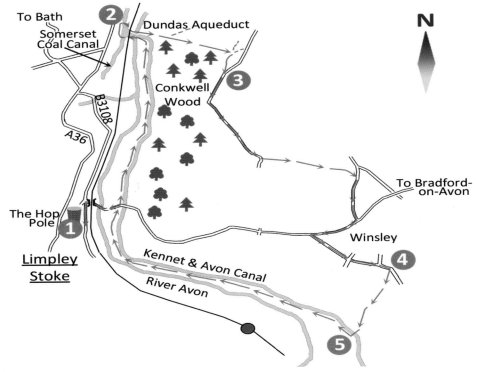

14. Savernake Forest

Paths, Pubs and Parking

Mainly level woodland walk.

There are picnic facilities within Savernake Forest but no actual pubs or restaurants. Marlborough is close by and offers a good choice of pubs, cafes and tearooms.

The walk begins at the car park at Postern Hill in the northwest corner of Savernake Forest (GR SU197682). From Marlborough take the A346 south towards Burbage. The entrance to the car park is on the left, heading south. Keep right at the immediate fork. Check the signs for opening times on arrival.

Royal Romance Amid the Glades

This glorious forest walk is best appreciated at the height of autumn when the dazzling colours of Savernake's numerous trees are truly awe-inspiring. The route never strays from the 2,300-acre forest and much of the time you are walking beneath a protective canopy of leaves and branches – perfect for shade from the sun or shelter from an unexpected downpour. One of the walk's key features is the forest's magnificent 4-mile Grand Avenue, which was planned by 'Capability' Brown who was also responsible for creating the forest you see today. Our route follows part of the Grand Avenue but essentially it is a journey to the heart of this great forest, renowned for its broad-leaved trees, tall pines, ancient pollarded oaks and much-loved beeches.

The Walk

1 With your back to the main road, walk ahead through the car park and picnic area, passing between trees, picnic tables and benches. Continue deep into the forest, eventually reaching a barrier and crossroads. Turn left. Look for a clearing over the left beyond the trees and on the right is a bridleway – **Church Walk**. Avoid it for now – the path crops up again later in the walk - and continue ahead, walking north with wooden fencing on the left. Pass a barrier and keep ahead to the A4.

2 Turn right along the grass verge and swing right to join **Grand Avenue**. Follow the tarmac drive between lines of stately beech trees. Pass a turning to **Braydon Oak** on the right and continue uphill. Pass several fields ringed by trees on the right. Beyond them the route reaches **Eight Walks**, as it is known, where eight tracks converge.

3 Take the first track on the right (**Great Lodge Drive**, a no through road) and follow it through picturesque parkland. Sheep may be seen grazing along here. The drive passes between trees once more and on the left is the entrance to **Thornhill Nursery**. Outbuildings are visible here. Drop down the hill and when the drive sweeps left, keep ahead beside a barrier and uphill on a footpath. The sound of traffic on the A346 is audible now. About 120 yards before you reach the road, look for a path on the left where the roof of a church can be seen through the trees. Take the path and soon you reach **Cadley church**, formerly a place of worship and now a private house. Return to the path junction near the A346, turn left and then almost immediately right to head north. This is **Church Walk**.

4 On reaching a fork by a grassy clearing, keep left and follow the path uphill to merge with another path. Continue uphill and keep left at the next fork. The sound of traffic on the A346 is audible. Cross over a track and follow a broad grassy path back to Postern Hill.

Savernake Forest's famous Grand Avenue

What to look out for

The forest views on this walk are superb – a delightful mix of sunny glades and peaceful, undisturbed woodland. It is here, in this tranquil setting, that you can allow your imagination to get working. Over the centuries, **Savernake's role as a working forest** was crucial to provide timber for shipbuilding and to play host to a succession of English kings as a royal hunting ground. It was William the Conqueror who appointed the first hereditary warden, Richard Esturmy, and it was one of his descendants who married into the Seymour family in the 15th century.

A clearing at Postern Hill

The Seymours then became wardens of Savernake. In 1535 Jane Seymour was introduced to Henry VIII while he was out hunting deer with her father, Sir John. According to tradition, Henry married Jane at Savernake. Her brother, Edward Seymour, was appointed warden around this time and was made Protector of the Realm, the Duke of Somerset, following Henry's death in 1547. Edward cleverly persuaded Henry's successor, Edward VI, to transfer the ownership of the estate to the Seymour family. In the second half of the 17th century, Savernake passed by marriage to the Bruce family and then to the current owner, the Marquess of Ailesbuy.

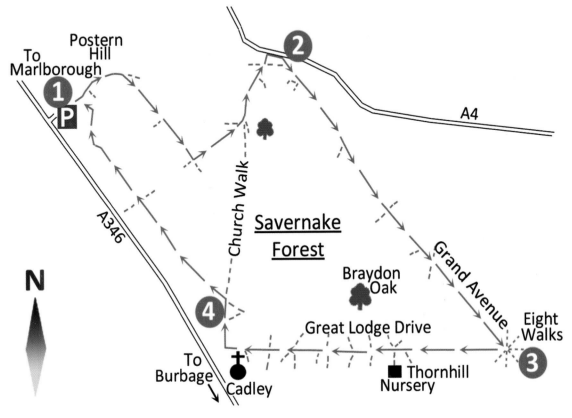

15. Castle Combe

From Poirot to War Horse

Voted the prettiest village in England in 1962 and set in a secluded wooded hollow, Castle Combe has all the ingredients to make it a tourist's dream: a market cross, a fast-flowing stream in the main street, a medieval packhorse bridge and the remains of a Norman castle. The village was once a prosperous centre of the wool trade, and became famous for its distinctive red and white cloth. Starting from the visitor car park, the walk is equally delightful, exploring an area of rolling countryside to the south of Castle Combe. Apart from two settlements, Ford and Long Dean, and an occasional stretch of road, the walk strenuously avoids obvious and intrusive reminders of the 20th century. Here and there, the route runs beside the By Brook, a tributary of the Avon.

The Walk

1 From the car park, make for some steps, turn right and walk down the lane towards **Castle Combe**. Keep right at the junction and pass the **Castle Inn** and the **White Hart**, following the road through the village. Pass over the **By Brook** and at this point there is a classic view of Castle Combe reproduced in thousands of postcards, calendars and tourist guides. Continue on the road with the brook running beside it and make for a footpath on the right, heading diagonally up the hillside.

2 Climb quite steeply through the trees and on reaching a woodland path at the top, bear left. Continue over the high ground to a stile and road and turn left. Shortly you come to a junction; turn right through a gate to join a path and then swing immediately left, initially following the path parallel to the road. The ground falls away dramatically to the right to reveal a delightful wooded dell. Cross a stile, emerging now onto open ground. Keep to the path as it traverses the upper slopes of the valley and on reaching a solitary waymark, keep right at the fork and descend the hillside to trees in the corner of the pasture. Make for a path threading through the trees and across the next pasture, down to the water's edge. Cross the brook via the footbridge, go over a stile stile and continue ahead in the field, keeping woodland on the right. In the corner follow a wide enclosed path through the trees. Cross a small field to a galvanized kissing gate between houses and follow the lane down to the main road (A420) at Ford.

3 Turn left along the road for a few paces, then left again to join the Castle Combe road by the entrance to **Bybrook Barn**. Follow it uphill between trees to a stile and path on the right. The grassy path, leading to **Long Dean**, curves gently round the hillside, in line with the contours and along here the scenery is a glorious mix of rolling pasture and valley. On reaching a stile, turn right and follow the path alongside a barbed wire fence. Following the **Macmillan Way**, go through a galvanized gate and follow a sunken path down to a lane at **Long Dean**. Pass over the **By Brook** and progress between several charming stone cottages.

Paths, Pubs and Parking

Picturesque undulating landscape with several ascents of varying grades.

The White Hart is one of several pubs in Castle Combe. There is also a tearoom in the village.

From Chippenham take the A420 west of the town and join the B4039. There is a large car park on the left, near Castle Combe. The walk begins here (GR ST845776).

Castle Combe's market cross

4 On reaching a junction with a post box in the wall, turn left and follow the track past Rose Cottage, heading uphill. At a fork keep right. Follow the green lane (Macmillan Way) towards Rack Hill, go over two stiles and continue on the clear route. Eventually you reach a footpath sign; just beyond it take the grassy path running half-right up the hill.

5 The path climbs to a kissing gate and then runs through extensive woodland with glimpses of Castle Combe and its church nestling in the hollow. When you come to a junction with a sunken path and a field opposite, turn left. At a fork reached after a few paces, you have a choice. To walk back into **Castle Combe**, keep left, to finish the walk and return to the car park, veer right. On the latter route, follow the sunken path down through the trees and emerge at the road opposite Hill House. Turn right and go uphill on the road, turning left for the car park.

The woods near the end of the walk

What to look out for

Considering its charm and pretty setting, it's hardly surprising that film and television location scouts have chosen Castle Combe for some major productions over the years. The first movie version of *Doctor Doolittle*, Hugh Lofting's children's classic, was shot here in 1967, though this adaptation was never a great success. Rex Harrison played the eponymous leading character and villagers were employed as extras at £2.50 a day. More than 40 years later, in September 2010, Steven Spielberg arrived in Castle Combe to film *War Horse*, and as a result the village was hurled back in time to the dark days of the Great War. Filming took ten days and Castle Combe church features a selection of photographs of scenes shot in the village. *The Murder of Roger Ackroyd*, a Poirot story with David Suchet playing the Belgian detective, was filmed here in 1999.

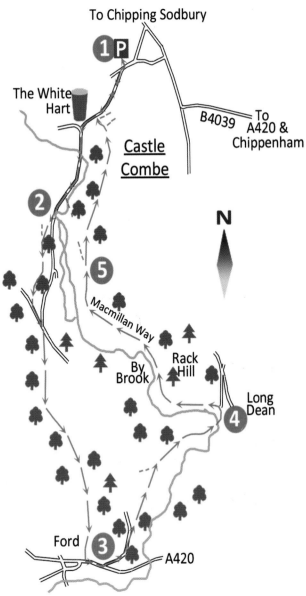

16. Old Wardour Castle

Paths, Pubs and Parking

Blend of river valley and undulating parkland. Some climbing but no dramatic ascents.

There are no pubs on the walk. A vending machine at the entrance to Old Wardour Castle offers tea, coffee and hot chocolate. Cold drinks, ice creams and pre-packed snacks are also available. For something more substantial, many of the towns and villages in the area have pubs and restaurants.

Take the A30 east of Shaftesbury, turning off to follow the signs for Old Wardour Castle. The walk begins in the adjacent car park (GR ST938264).

In the Shadow of a Romantic Ruin

This is a very enjoyable walk in any season but particularly so on a dark winter's day when the setting is highly evocative and atmospheric. In the fading light of a December or January day the remains of Old Wardour Castle lend an air of mystery and menace and the place is so quiet and peaceful you could almost hear a pin drop. From the site the route explores part of the tranquil Nadder Valley, cutting through woodland and across rolling parkland to New Wardour Castle before returning to the start.

The Walk

1 From the car park turn left along the drive, passing between **Cresswell's Pond** and the remains of **Old Wardour Castle**. Pass the **Gothic Pavilion** and at **Wardour House** soon after it, bear right to follow the track, climbing gently. Keep to the right of woodland, avoid a track running off to the right and continue alongside the trees. Over to the right in the distance is the outline of **New Wardour Castle**, a Palladian mansion. Keep right at a fork by a stone archway and make for the corner of the wood where the route reaches a gateway leading into a field. Walk ahead along its right-hand edge, keeping fencing on the right. Head for a gateway in the bottom right-hand corner of the pasture and cross over into the trees. **Pale Park Pond** is visible on the left.

2 Follow the path beside it and on reaching a kissing gate by a sign for the **Wessex Ridgeway**, head up the field slope towards trees. Make for a gate leading into further woodland and after about 60 yards, bear right to follow a track. Continue along to a fork, keeping right along the lower track. On reaching a Forestry Commission sign for **Wardour Wood**, pass a barrier and follow the drive. Continue to the end of the hedge by a gateway and turn right over a stile. Drop down the field slope, keeping right to a gate and stile in the trees. Follow the path through the copse and on reaching a grassy clearing, bear left, heading down to a wrought iron gate and squeeze stile, with a footpath sign. Keep to the right-hand edge of the field towards **Park Gate Farm**.

3 Cross the stile and track into the concrete farmyard to a small gate. Walk along the path with a high laurel ledge to your left and field to the right and exit at the next small gate. Over to your left the **River Nadder** meanders through the pastoral Wiltshire countryside. Make for the far right corner of the pasture and cross a stile leading into the next field. Go diagonally up the slope, keeping to the left of a cottage. Cross two stiles with a farm road in between and head up the grassy hillside to trees. Aim for a stile in the boundary and keep right at the fork beyond it. Pass a stone house on the left and as you emerge from the trees, **New Wardour Castle** looms in front of you. At the next fork, keep left alongside a fence and continue beside laurel bushes and hedging. Bear right at a path junction to take the third exit, heading towards New Wardour Castle, with fencing on the left.

The atmospheric remains of Old Wardour Castle

4 Pass along the front of the building and beside a parking area and continue to a fork. Keep right, aim for a stile and gate and follow the grassy parkland track towards **Old Wardour Castle**. Head down to a stile and galvanized gate, bear right and at the next junction, turn left and retrace your steps to the start.

What to look out for

Old Wardour Castle, which dates back to the end of the 14th century, was built for John, 5th Lord Lovel of Titchmarsh, and remodelled in 1578. What sets Wardour

Cresswell's Pond

apart from other fortifications around the country is its hexagonal shape. Its rooms and chambers are all contained within the one main building, which also makes it unique. After the Civil War Wardour was abandoned and fell into disrepair. In 1991 it was chosen as Locksley Castle, the family home of Robin Hood, in the film *Robin Hood: Prince of Thieves*, starring Kevin Costner in the title role.

Snowdrops line the route in places in the early weeks of the year – usually for most of the month of February. The drooping white flowers of this instantly recognizable bulbous plant add a touch of colour and brightness to long winter days, and their appearance is a reminder that spring is on the way.

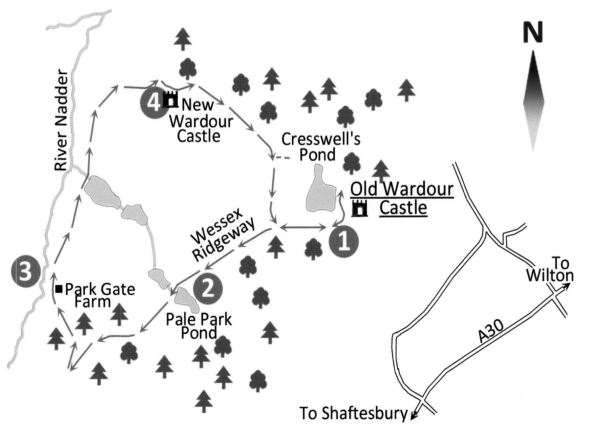

17. Stonehenge

Paths, Pubs and Parking

Tracks, paths, quiet country roads and one stretch of pavement alongside the A345.

There are no pubs on the route of the walk. However, there is a cafeteria at the Stonehenge visitor centre, and nearby Amesbury includes several pubs and restaurants.

To reach Woodhenge, where the walk begins, follow the A345 north of Amesbury. The turning for the site and car park is on the left beyond lines of houses (GR SU151433).

Discovering Wiltshire's Distant Past

Stonehenge is one of Britain's most intriguing and enigmatic ancient landmarks. A World Heritage Site of unique importance and interest and surrounded by ceremonial and domestic structures, this major tourist attraction is on every foreign tourist's list of places to visit in this country and often at the very top. Winter is often a good time to walk here, when the weather conditions can add to the drama and lend the place an even darker sense of mystery. However, the summer is also ideal for exploring Stonehenge's surroundings on foot and if you happen to be here for the solstice on 21 June, the longest day of the calendar, you'll find the place teeming with all manner of visitors, many of them dressed as Druids. The reason? Stonehenge is perfectly aligned with the points of sunrise and sunset. Witnessing the sunrise over this awesome site on a beautiful summer's day – or indeed seeing it set on 21 December, the shortest day – is an extraordinarily magical and humbling experience. From the parking area at Woodhenge, the walk heads south and then west to follow what is believed to be an ancient processional route to Stonehenge. From the stones, the walk runs north to Larkhill and then across country back to Woodhenge. Situated roughly midway round the walk, Stonehenge is an outstanding feature in the Wiltshire landscape and a unique point of interest. As you mingle with the thousands of international visitors peering at the stones or perhaps relax over a coffee in the cafeteria, you might reflect that few people, if any, that day will have come to Stonehenge as part of a circular country walk.

The Walk

1 From the parking area at **Woodhenge**, originally a wooden structure set up during the Bronze Age for ceremonial use, follow the road back towards the A345. Bear right before the junction and cut between bollards to follow a track, which soon narrows to a path and then merges with the main road. Follow the A345 south towards **Amesbury**, at one point crossing from the right-hand pavement to the left one. Continue to where a waymarked track (**King Barrows, Cursus and Larkhill**) can be seen running off to the right. Take the turning. Pass a line of electricity pylons and soon the track reaches a wooden signpost on the right (**Old King Barrows**). Keep on the track as it bears left, following it in a straight line for about ¾ mile. The track eventually bends right to a junction.

2 Turn left after a short distance, following the track signposted to **King Barrows**. Bend left and continue beyond trees and fields lining the route to reach a gate on the right. Pass through it and in the distance is the outline of **Stonehenge** nestling amid the downland. There is no obvious path on this stretch of the walk but keep roughly straight ahead, dropping down the grassy slope towards **Stonehenge Bottom**. Aim for a gate in the next boundary. Keep ahead for about 75 yards to a junction of paths and an information panel explaining the significance of Stonehenge Avenue. Take the first left path and ahead on the skyline are the ancient stones, dramatic and breathtaking in any season. As you approach the stones, with fencing in front of them, bear right and follow a grassy path along the boundary to a gate giving

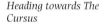
Heading towards The Cursus

access to a broad byway. Shuttle buses can be seen on the left. To visit **Stonehenge**, first walk along designated paths to the visitor centre 1½ miles to the north (or catch the bus), buy your ticket and then return to this point.

3 To continue the walk, follow the byway away from the stones towards **Larkhill** and the **Cursus**. On the left is **Stonehenge Down**. Head north on the track, cutting between fences with stunning, far-reaching views of remote Wiltshire downland. Keep on the track towards trees, cross the **Cursus**, a 1.7-mile ditch built with the use of antler picks about 5,500 years ago, and follow the byway beside belts of woodland. At this stage of the walk, the bustle of visitors to Stonehenge begins to recede. Over to the right are the buildings of **Durrington Down Farm**. At the next main

Along the way

junction, turn right along **Fargo Road** with the houses of **Larkhill** on the left. Follow the road out into a patch of countryside. Glancing to the right reveals a final view of **Stonehenge** in the distance. Continue on the road to the next row of houses. Pass alongside them and as the road bears left, turn right by a 20-mph sign and a bus shelter to follow a track.

4 Pass between paddocks to a gate and track junction. Turn left here and follow the path. On reaching woodland on the left, turn left for several paces to a post. Turn right at this point and walk beside the trees. At the next corner of the woodland, turn left by a fence (signposted Larkhill 1½ miles). Keep fencing on the right and follow the path to the next road. Turn right by some houses and follow the road between fields, back to the start at **Woodhenge**.

What to look out for

The exact purpose of **Stonehenge** and how this stone circle originated are mysteries shrouded in the mists of time. Trying to solve the great riddle is one of the reasons more than a million visitors make the pilgrimage here every year. However, erosion and the threat of damage have resulted in restricted access to the stones and these days an enclosed path circles the site, offering visitors the chance for close-up views and photographs. English Heritage do run tours that give visitors direct access to the stones but you need to apply in good time as they are immensely popular.

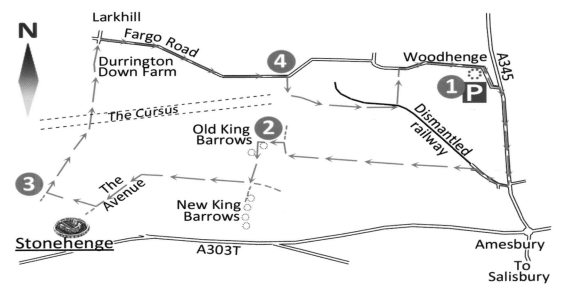

18. Honeystreet

Paths, Pubs and Parking

Canal towpath, field paths and tracks, quiet stretches of road. Because the route is on low ground expect to encounter some muddy patches.

The Barge at Honeystreet, where the walk begins, occupies a very pleasant canalside setting, making it an obvious destination for thirsty walkers and cyclists. The pub has been a brewery, bakery, village store and slaughterhouse at different times over the years. The garden is especially popular with customers in good weather. For an alternative menu, try the Honeystreet Café near the start of the walk.

The hamlet of Honeystreet lies southwest of Marlborough, between the A345 and the A361. Make for the village of Alton Barnes and keep ahead to cross the Kennet & Avon Canal at Honeystreet. Turn immediately right for the Barge and follow the access road to the car park (GR SU101615).

In Search of a Saxon Church and a Chalk Horse

Many walks in this scenic corner of Wiltshire head for the dramatic escarpment of the downs above the Kennet & Avon Canal. However, this gentle route strenuously avoids steep ascents and demanding climbs by keeping to low ground close to the waterway. From the Barge at Honeystreet the walk makes for neighbouring Alton Barnes before heading west, south and then east, back to the Kennet & Avon. Along the way, particularly in the early stages of the walk, there are spectacular views of the Vale of Pewsey, where there is a strong sense of Wiltshire's ancient history.

The Walk

1 Join the towpath by the **Barge at Honeystreet** and turn right. Walk alongside the **Kennet & Avon Canal** to **bridge 124**, then, at the side of it, follow the path up to the road. Turn left and walk towards **Alton Barnes**. Turn right at the sign for **St Mary's Saxon church** and after several hundred yards pass a turnstile and a paved path on the left. This is part of the **White Horse Trail**. Continue to St Mary's church. Restored during the Victorian era, St Mary's has a timber roof, a Saxon nave and engraved glass panels by Laurence Whistler. Retrace your steps to the T-junction. Turn left for several steps, turning right at the footpath sign into a field.

2 Head out across open farmland, with good views of the **Alton Barnes White Horse** up on the hillside. Make for a stile and over to the left is the outline of the Barge at Honeystreet. Continue across the next field and on reaching a bridleway on the far side, aim for a lane just a short distance away over to the left. Walk down to it, reaching the lane on a bend, and keep left at this point. Pass several houses and bungalows and at the junction, keep left. Follow the lane in a southerly direction, with good views of distant downland.

3 Cross the Kennet & Avon at **Stanton Bridge** and continue on the lane between hedges and fields. Pass the entrance to **Mill Farm**, swing left by a gateway and after about 100 yards, the road bends right at a sign for **Stanton Farm**. Turn left here to follow a bridleway between farmland. From the track there are good views of the White Horse and its surrounding downland. Follow the track round several bends, avoid a turning on the right and continue on a lengthy, straight stretch. On reaching some corrugated barns, follow the track for a few paces to a waymarked junction. Go straight on and at the road turn left.

4 Continue to a right-hand bridlepath, following it down to trees and bushes. Keep on the right of way as it curves

The Kennet & Avon Canal at Honeystreet

right, then left. Skirt a field, keeping alongside fencing, and at the top of the gentle slope, you reach the **Kennet & Avon towpath**. Turn left, walk along to the signposted Second World War memorial in the field on the left and then continue to the next bridge (**123**). Keep beside the waterway as it curves left, with good views over spacious Wiltshire downland. Pass under **bridge 124** and return to the **Barge at Honeystreet** where the walk began.

The Alton Barnes White Horse seen from the route

What to look out for

The **Alton Barnes White Horse**, a chalk figure carved into the hillside, was cut in 1812 and is one of many similar striking carvings throughout the county. These instantly recognizable and wonderfully timeless landmarks were created in honour of the horse, man's much-loved travelling companion – loyal, dependable, trustworthy and hardworking. Measuring 166ft by 160ft, the **Alton Barnes White Horse** was cut by a man who absconded with his £20 fee before finishing the job. He was later caught and hanged.

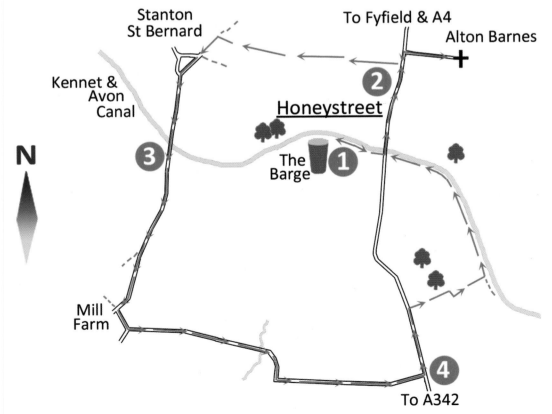

19. Barbury Castle

Paths, Pubs and Parking

This is a vey exposed walk over expansive downland so protective clothing is recommended. Mainly ancient paths and well-used tracks with several brief climbs.

There are no pubs or cafes on the actual route. However, there are various villages in the vicinity of the walk offering a good selection of refreshments. Try the Honey Pot Café at Wroughton (reached to the west of Chiseldon along the B4005), which includes a variety of snacks and meals.

The walk starts at Barbury Castle Country Park (GR SU156760). Take the A346 between Marlborough and junction 15 of the M4, turning off at Chiseldon to join the B4005. Follow the signs for Barbury Castle, heading south and uphill to the car park.

Ancient Earthworks Amid Dramatic Downland

The breathtaking Wessex downs of Wiltshire inspire a marvellous sense of space and freedom, as well as providing a fascinating window on our past. The vast downland country between Marlborough and Swindon, known as the Marlborough Downs, is just the place for an invigorating walk with a strong hint of ancient history. The route begins at Barbury Castle and then explores the remote landscape to its north. At times you really feel you are walking in the footsteps of the people of the Bronze Age and Iron Age. This swathe of open downland is littered with burial mounds, field monuments and ancient hill forts.

The Walk

1 Go to the far western end of the car park, pass public conveniences and make for a gate. There is a sign here 'to the hill-fort'. Keep ahead on the **Ridgeway** towards the eastern end of the **Barbury Castle earthworks**. Go through the gate and walk ahead through its centre with ditches and ramparts either side of you. Take the obvious path downhill to a lane and turn right.

2 Follow the lane for about 50 yards and then turn right again to follow a track. Keep on this all the way to the next road junction. Turn left for about 50 yards, swinging right to join a byway. Follow the wide track, passing beside trees. Continue to the next hedgerow on the right, running at right angles to the track. Take the path here, following it to **Barbury Castle** via **Burderop Down**.

3 Follow the field edge with hedgerow on the left, passing a dilapidated barn. Make for a waymark at the end of a line of trees and follow the path left. Swing right after a few paces towards a gap in the trees on the brow of the hill and pass a **Millennium Trail** sign. Follow the bridleway in line with the contours and when you reach a junction with a track turn sharp right to join a byway.

4 Go through the gate and soon you start climbing towards **Burderop Down**. The ascent is quite steep. On the crest of the hill continue on the

The wonderful Wessex downs

track. Keep ahead and to the north are glorious views over a sprawling Wiltshire landscape. Swindon can be seen in the distance. Over on the right is a memorial stone to two literary figures – Richard Jefferies and Alfred Williams. Keep on the track and on reaching the lane, turn left and return to the car park where the walk began.

What to look out for

Barbury Castle, which covers about 12 acres, is a large Iron Age fort defended by ditches and a double bank. The site may have been re-fortified in Saxon times, as previous excavations have produced evidence of a lengthy and continuous period of occupation. Finds here include flint axes, weapons, tools, jewellery and Iron Age and Roman pottery.

The Ridgeway National Trail, encountered at the start of the walk, runs for 85 miles between Avebury and Ivinghoe Beacon in Buckinghamshire. The route follows Britain's oldest road, originally used for trade, much of it traversing open and exposed chalk downland.

The view from the Ridgeway

Richard Jefferies and **Alfred Williams** – whose names are commemorated on a stone near the end of the walk – are still remembered in Wiltshire. Jefferies, a 19th century writer and journalist, wrote: 'They only know a country who are acquainted with its footpaths. By the roads, indeed, the outside may be seen; but the footpaths go through the heart of the land. '

Alfred Williams is recalled in Walk 10 at South Marston.

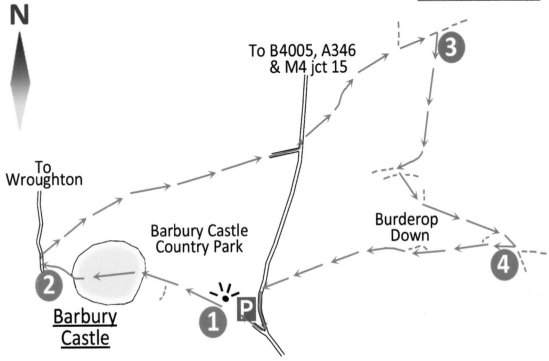

N

To B4005, A346 & M4 jct 15

③

To Wroughton

Barbury Castle Country Park

Burderop Down

④

②

Barbury Castle

①

P

20. Malmesbury

A Town Tour and a Water Meadows Walk

This short walk is just right in the depths of winter - short but long enough to feel the benefit and with the added promise of a log fire and something to eat or drink in one of the town pubs at the end of it. Much of the route is within the boundaries of Malmesbury, which John Betjeman described as "a perfect English medieval limestone town", but there are stretches across fields and meadows and beside the Tetbury and Sherston branches of the River Avon. The town is never far away and here and there the walk offers splendid views of its period buildings and magnificent Norman abbey.

The Walk

1 Walk to the far end of the car park and turn right at the sign for town centre, toilets and **Abbey House Gardens**. Cross the river bridge and then head up a flight of steps to **Malmesbury Abbey**. Pass through to the road and make for the **Market Cross** in the centre of the town. With your back to it, turn right along **Gloucester Street** and when it bends right, go straight on down the slope (**King's Walk**).

2 When the path forks, keep right and descend steps. At the bottom turn right along **Burnivale** and swing left to join a public footpath. Cross the bridge and then follow the riverside path to a meadow. Cross another branch of the Avon and keep ahead, avoiding the path on the immediate left. Pass through a gap in the wall and hedge and glance over to your left at this point for a very pleasant view of Malmesbury, with its historic abbey and church on the skyline. Follow the field edge path with hedge on the left and houses beyond, make for the corner and go through a kissing gate and across a wooden footbridge. Continue in the next field, still with the boundary on your immediate left. Follow the path to the next footbridge and gate, with the river just down below. Cross several more footbridges and a kissing gate and continue on the waterside path. **Avon Mills** is visible as you approach the road.

3 Cross a stile, go through a gate and then turn left at the road. Cross the Avon at the footbridge and at the path junction on the far side, bear right for the road. Cross over into **St John Street** and continue to a bridge. Cross it and walk along **Baskerville**, passing **Malmesbury Bowls Club**. Turn left immediately before **Wynyard Mill** to follow a footpath. Cross a footbridge and stile and continue along the edge of meadows with the Avon on your immediate right. Make for the corner of the meadows, turning right to a gate and stile and the remains of a disused railway line, which closed in 1962. Continue in the next meadow, near where the river divides, and make for a road on the far side. Cross a stile and go up several steps to reach it.

4 Continue on the opposite side of the road, following a woodland path with the river on your left. This is part of **Conygre Mead Nature Reserve**. Keep ahead through the woods, the path following the route of the former Malmesbury to Dauntsey railway line. At the latter station the track connected with the main line between London and Bristol. The line was built by Richard Ward, an

Paths, Pubs and Parking

Water shadows you all the way on this walk. The going is easy, especially in the town itself. However, expect some muddy patches in the surrounding fields, meadows and woodland.

Malmesbury benefits from a number of pubs and several cafes and tearooms. One of the town's oldest and most popular inns is the Smoking Dog located in the High Street.

Malmesbury is on the A429, north of junction 17 of the M4. The walk begins at the Station car park (fee-paying) on the north side of the town, off the B4014 (GR ST933874).

Malmesbury's fine 15th-century market cross

engineer and former apprentice of Brunel. Along the Conygre Mead stretch you can see where the track crossed the river before entering a tunnel. Soon you reach the car park where the walk began.

What to look out for

Perched high on a rocky promontory, **Malmesbury** is one of Wiltshire's most fascinating towns. But there is far more to the place than its attractive setting and wonderful sense of history. A short tour illustrates an Anglo-Saxon street plan and a town wall. More than anything, Malmesbury is a perfect example of a Saxon fortified hilltop town

The River Avon flowing through Malmesbury

dating back to about AD 600. Later, in AD 880, Alfred granted the town a charter and constructed defences after recapturing Malmesbury from the Vikings. The abbey, which legend suggests was founded by a Celtic monk, was once the town's parish church, distinguished by a square tower surmounted by a spire, supposedly higher than that of Salisbury Cathedral. The tower collapsed during a storm in about 1500. At the Dissolution of the Monasteries, Malmesbury Abbey was sold to a clothier for little more than £1,500. Thereafter, Malmesbury's fortunes began to improve markedly and, thanks to an endless supply of water around the town, it became an important centre for the manufacture of woollen cloth, lace and silk. Most of the 18th century buildings you see today reflect that chapter in the town's economy.

Conygre Mead Nature Reserve is rich in wildlife and includes 170 plant species, 18 types of butterflies and various breeding birds. On the slopes grow native wild flowers such as common knapweed.

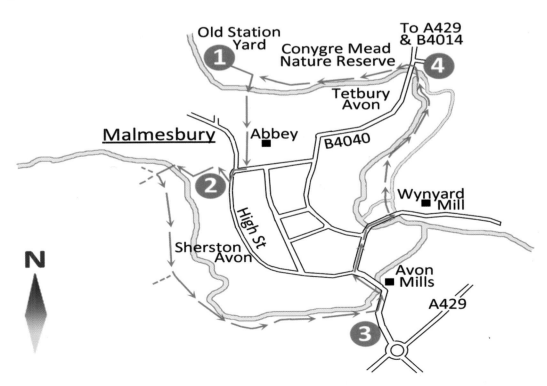

The historic Kennet & Avon Canal in high summer (Walk 8)